The Leadership Challenge Planner

AN ACTION GUIDE TO ACHIEVING YOUR PERSONAL BEST

James M. Kouzes

Barry Z. Posner

JOSSEY-BASS/PFEIFFER
A Wiley Company
www.pfeiffer.com

D0818167

Published by

JOSSEY-BASS/PFEIFFER

A Wiley Company
989 Market Street
San Francisco, CA 94103-1741
415.433.1740; Fax 415.433.0499
800.274.4434; Fax 800.569.0443

www.pfeiffer.com

ISBN: 0-7879-4568-4
Library of Congress Catalog Card Number 99-071499

Acquiring Editor: Larry Alexander
Director of Development: Kathleen Dolan Davies
Developmental Editor: Lynn Parode
Project Manager: Rachel Livsey
Senior Production Editor: Pamela Berkman
Senior Manufacturing Supervisor: Becky Carreño
Interior Design: Yvo Riezebos
Cover Design: Beth Loudenberg
Illustrations: Richard Sheppard

Visit our website at: www.pfeiffer.com

Printed in the United States of America

We at Jossey-Bass/Pfeiffer strive to use the most environmentally sensitive paper stocks available to us.
Our publications are printed on acid-free recycled stock whenever possible, and our paper always meets or
exceeds minimum GPO and EPA requirements.

Jossey-Bass/Pfeiffer also publishes its books in a variety of electronic formats. Some content that appears
in print may not be available in electronic books.

Printing   10   9   8   7   6

The Leadership
Challenge Planner

Contents

CONTENTS

Acknowledgments

ACKNOWLEDGMENTS

When we seek out the wellspring of our various published works, we invariably discover a group of eager and committed learners who are always thirsty for more practical knowledge. "How do we put this into practice?" they persistently ask. *The Leadership Challenge Planner* sprang from this well. We owe the most gratitude to our past and present participants in The Leadership Challenge Workshops, for their constant supply of new ideas and for continually requesting materials they can use.

We've always thought of the *five practices of exemplary leadership* as both a process for planning change and a set of skills for guiding change. To help people use the five practices as a guide to change, we initially wrote a ten-page list of probing questions that walked people step-by-step through a real-life change initiative. With the constant encouragement and persistence of our colleagues at the Tom Peters Group/Learning Systems—who kept asking us for something our customers could use on their pressing problems at home—the initial list of questions was transformed into "The Next Personal Best Planner." It's become an indispensable part of The Leadership Challenge Workshops. Christy Tonge was the primary author of that tool; her soaring talent inspires everyone she works with. Working in collaboration with Christy were Cathy Weselby, an instructional designer extraordinaire, and Homi Eshaghi, our master of graphics design.

Overseeing the original planner was Lynne Parode. Lynne brought to the project her talent as an instructional designer and writer in her own right, and her immense capacity and tenacity to manage the process of turning an idea into print. When it came time to transform a workshop tool into a self-directed guidebook, we turned to Lynne again for her expertise. We are blessed that Lynne could share her energy with us, and the instructional design of *The Leadership Challenge Planner* is the product of her shining talent. Lynne cocreated this book, and we thank her for devoting her passion and intellect to this project.

As is true with all of our most recent publications, Rachel Livsey, project manager of the Leadership Challenge products for our publishers, Jossey-Bass and Jossey-Bass/Pfeiffer, is responsible for making sure that this book first made it into manuscript and then was transformed into a book. Rachel is an indispensable member of our team, and without her we'd be lost in the publisher's wilderness. We also want to thank Larry Alexander, who developed the initial idea and signed the contracts for this book. And special thanks to Lisa Shannon, who convinced her colleagues at Jossey-Bass that *The Leadership Challenge Planner* was worthy of trade-book status. We are grateful for her confidence in us.

Finally, our thanks to every one of you who want to continue to pursue your leadership dreams and advance your personal skills. Never forget that you make a difference.

The Authors

T H E   A U T H O R S

JAMES M. KOUZES is chairman of the Tom Peters Group/Learning Systems, which makes leadership work through practical, performance-oriented learning programs, including The Leadership Challenge Workshop and Leadership Is Everyone's Business. In 1993 the *Wall Street Journal* cited him as one of the twelve most requested "nonuniversity executive-education providers" to U.S. companies.

BARRY Z. POSNER, Ph.D., is dean of the Leavey School of Business, Santa Clara University, and professor of organizational behavior. He has received several outstanding teaching and leadership awards, has published more than eighty research and practitioner-oriented articles, and currently is on the editorial review boards for the *Journal of Management Education,* the *Journal of Management Inquiry,* and the *Journal of Business Ethics.* He also serves on the board of directors for Public Allies-Silicon Valley and for the Center for Excellence in Nonprofits.

Both are renowned speakers and leadership developers who have conducted programs for 3M, Arthur Andersen, Applied Materials, AT&T, Boy Scouts of America, Bank of America, Charles Schwab, Ciba-Geigy, Dell Computer, Federal Express, Honeywell, Johnson and Johnson, Levi Strauss, L. L. Bean, Lockheed Martin, Merck, Motorola, MTV, Sun Microsystems, Toshiba, TRW, Xerox, and the YMCA, among other organizations.

Kouzes and Posner are coauthors of several best-selling and award-winning leadership books. *The Leadership Challenge: How to Keep Getting Extraordinary Things Done in Organizations* (second edition 1995), with more than eight hundred thousand copies in print, has been reprinted in fifteen foreign languages, featured in three video programs, and received a Critic's Choice award from the nation's newspaper book review editors. *Credibility: How Leaders Gain and Lose It, Why People Demand It* (1993) was chosen by *Industry Week* as one of the five best management books of the year. Their most recent book *Encouraging the Heart* (1999) is on its way to being another bestseller. Kouzes and Posner also developed the *Leadership Practices Inventory (LPI)* (second edition 1997), a valid and reliable 360 degree feedback instrument that measures leadership behavior. It is one of the most-used leadership inventories in the world, having been completed by nearly one million leaders and constituents. In addition to the LPI's manager, individual-contributor, and team versions, a student version of the *Leadership Practices Inventory* was recently released.

Introduction

INTRODUCTION

When we interviewed Don Bennett for our first book, *The Leadership Challenge,* he said something that we've never forgotten. Bennett is the first amputee to climb Mt. Rainier. That's 14,410 feet on one leg and two crutches.

"How did you make it to the top?" we asked Bennett.

"One hop at a time," was his instant reply.

One hop at a time. One hop at a time. One hop at a time.

When you think about it, that's how most change is accomplished. Yet we sometimes find ourselves simply paralyzed by the pace of change. We're challenged to do more with less, adapt quickly to changing circumstances, and somehow still find time for our families and friends. Sometimes it's all just too overwhelming. But so is looking up to the top of that mountain when you're at the bottom. That's why Bennett would tell himself, as he looked just one foot ahead, "Anybody can hop from here to there." And so he did—fourteen thousand four hundred ten times.

After being asked over and over again by our clients and students how to prepare for change, we decided that it was time to produce a guide to assist leaders in using the five practices of exemplary leadership model as a tool for planning. *The Leadership Challenge Planner* is a one-hop-at-a-time workbook for leaders. It's designed to help you reflect and act on your need (or your organization's) for change.

What Are the Five Practices of Exemplary Leadership and a "Personal Best"?

Every new project you take on is an opportunity for greatness—for attaining a personal best that defines your own standard of excellence. It is through leading important and challenging projects, in fact, that leaders "get extraordinary things done" in organizations. Your next major project is your chance not only to create extraordinary results for your organization but also to develop your leadership capabilities. This planner helps you do both.

When we began our research, we decided to find out what practices characterize exemplary leaders: people who get extraordinary things done in organizations. Our research began with analyzing what behaviors people demonstrated when they were leading a project that they considered a "personal best": one that set an individual standard of excellence for them. We collected thousands of stories of leaders performing at their peak, and we looked at what actions seemed to be consistent in all the stories. Several years—and several thousand quantitative and qualitative analyses—later, we found that five practices define exemplary leadership:

1. Challenging the process
2. Inspiring a shared vision
3. Enabling others to act
4. Modeling the way
5. Encouraging the heart

Our research is described in detail in our book *The Leadership Challenge* (published by Jossey-Bass). We found that you can improve your effectiveness as a leader to the extent that you can engage in these five practices more consistently than you do at present. You may have already read *The Leadership Challenge* or used *The Leadership Practices Inventory* (*LPI*) to further your development as a leader. The *LPI* provides valuable feedback on how you are currently doing in these five areas, in the eyes of those you work with most closely. It can help you target areas needing improvement and identify specific actions to improve your effectiveness.

Who Should Use *The Leadership Challenge Planner*?

The purpose of this planner is to assist people, managers and nonmanagers alike, in furthering their ability to lead others and get extraordinary things done. Whether you're in the private or public sector, an employee or a volunteer, on the front lines or in the senior echelon, a student or a parent, by completing this planner you develop your leadership skills and guide others to places you (and they) have never been before. We believe that you're capable of developing yourself as a leader far more than tradition or mythology has ever assumed possible.

Leadership isn't about being in a formal position. Rather, it's about having the courage and spirit to move from whatever circumstances you're in so as to make a significant difference. And you don't even need to be called a "leader" to achieve extraordinary things in your organization. This planner is designed to help anyone achieve his or her personal best on a project that innovates and changes the organization—anyone, that is, who has the desire to make a difference.

Achieving Your Personal Best

The *Planner* is a powerful tool for your leadership development. It's designed to help you create and accomplish your personal best in a specific project you're about to undertake. You use it to think through the requirements and challenges of the project, and then you plan how to carry out the five practices that lead others to successfully complete the project.

We hope that this planner convinces you that leadership is everyone's business. The next time you say to yourself, *Why don't they do something about this?* look in the mirror. Ask the person you see, *Why don't you do something about this?* By accepting the challenge to lead, you come to realize that the only limits are those you place on yourself. Imagine yourself standing at the base of Mt. Rainier, and then start climbing—one hop at a time.

The Leadership Challenge Planner enables you to unleash more of your own courage and more of your own talent to achieve your personal best.

Now, onward and upward!

JAMES M. **K O U Z E S**

Palo Alto, California

BARRY Z. *P O S N E R*

Santa Clara, California

February 1999

1 How to Use This Planner

We'd like you to begin *The Leadership Challenge Planner* by selecting an upcoming project to target as an opportunity to do your personal best.

As you work through each practice individually, this planner supports your success on three levels:

1. **Reflection**. One of its roles is to get you to think a little differently about how you approach the project. The questions posed are designed to challenge your thinking and broaden your perspective.

2. **Intention**. All great accomplishments start with deep commitment. Practical exercises help you think through how you intend to bring each leadership practice forward in your chosen project.

3. **Action**. In the concluding section, we provide useful tools for translating your intentions into consistent action. Each week, you map out your interim goals for the project and list actions you'll take to demonstrate each of the five practices.

On a practical level, we recommend that you complete most or all of the *Planner* prior to starting the project. You may choose to work through the five practices in the order we've presented them, or you may want to start with the practice you're most interested in developing. You may find that some questions are richer and more useful to you than others. We encourage you to proceed through this book in whatever way resonates for you.

We do encourage you to take a stab at all the activities, though, and complete the "bottom line" exercise at the end of each of the five chapters on leadership practices (three through seven); in these exercises, you commit to taking several action steps. Once these are completed, you transfer those action steps to your "grand plan," in Chapter Eight. As the project proceeds, you create weekly plans (also in Chapter Eight), referring back to your grand plan and adjusting as needed. Every day, you'll want to use the weekly plan to remind yourself of the leadership actions you intend to weave into progress on your project.

Once your project is well under way (or after it's finished), we strongly encourage you to complete the work in Chapter Nine, "Reflecting on Your Personal Best Project." Those questions take you through a debriefing in which you reflect on the highs and lows of your project and what you learned—lessons you can then go on to apply to your next personal best project.

2 Selecting Your Personal Best Project

You're using this planner to think through one specific upcoming project that you'll lead. For this effort to be meaningful, we recommend working on a project that:

- Is about to start or has just started

- Represents a significant challenge for you

- Is important to you and your organization, group, or team

Take a few minutes to reflect on your leadership role—whether formal or informal, appointed, selected, or self-initiated—and the various projects (impending or just initiated) that might meet these three criteria. It doesn't have to be a project at the office. Remember what we said in the beginning: leadership is everyone's business. Your project can be one that involves your community, religious organization, volunteer association, or your work. You'll find that you can use this planner for all kinds of change initiatives. Here are some examples of projects that are appropriate subjects:

- You are trying to institute a new system or process and expect to face some resistance.

- You've volunteered to lead a community improvement effort and folks are apathetic, or even cynical.

- You've been promoted or given new responsibilities.

- You're taking over a project from someone else midstream. (This planner is especially appropriate for a project that got off track.)

- You need to grow business this quarter despite limited resources.

- You're creating a new event: a program, publication, association, or something no one has ever done before.

- You're responsible for helping the team meet a difficult deadline.

- You're opening a new territory or launching a new product.

Use Worksheet One, "My Personal Best Project," to describe the challenge in detail.

MY PERSONAL BEST PROJECT

Describe the challenge you've selected to work through in this planner.

What are the project goals?

What's the time frame?

What's the budget?

Who is on the project team? What are their titles, positions, and roles? What do you know about each person that's relevant to the project's success?

What other actual or virtual team members should you include? (Consider customers and vendors, for example.)

Who are the stakeholders in the success of the project? What criteria do they use to measure success? (Complete the grid below.)

Stakeholder	Criteria for Success
me	

What are your current feelings regarding this project? List several nouns, such as *excitement, dread, panic, anticipation,* etc.

What aspects of this project do you expect to be frustrating or difficult? List the specific aspects of this undertaking that are most challenging.

Why is this project important . . .

(1) To you?

(2) To your organization?

(3) To anyone else (for example, the community, stockholders, other departments, colleagues, etc.)?

In the next five chapters, you explore the five leadership practices in turn, with a focus on expanding and enhancing your own leadership practices as you lead this project. We believe these pages will be instrumental in your achieving a personal best.

3 Challenging the Process

LEADERS VENTURE OUT. Although many people in our studies attributed their success to "luck" or "being in the right place at the right time," none of them sat idly waiting for fate to smile upon them. Those who lead others to greatness seek and accept challenge.

Every single personal best leadership case we collected involved some kind of challenge. Whatever the challenge, all the cases involved change from the status quo, which is to say, of course, that not one person claimed to have done his or her personal best by keeping things the same. In short, **ALL LEADERS CHALLENGE THE PROCESS.**

LEADERS ARE PIONEERS: people who are willing to step out into the unknown. They're willing to take risks, innovate, and experiment to find new and better ways of doing things. But leaders need not always be the creators or originators of new products, services, or processes. In fact, it's just as likely that they're not. In reality, product and service innovations tend to come not from leaders but from customers, clients, vendors, people in the labs, and people on the front lines, while process innovations usually come from the people who are doing the work.

So it may be a dramatic external event that thrusts us into a radically new condition. The leader's primary contribution is in recognizing good ideas, supporting them, and being willing to challenge the system to get new products, processes, services, and systems adopted. It might be more accurate, then, to say that **LEADERS ARE EARLY ADOPTERS OF INNOVATION.** Leaders know well that experimentation, innovation, and change all involve risk and failure—but they proceed anyway.

It would be ridiculous to assert that those who fail over and over again eventually succeed as leaders. Success in any endeavor isn't a process of simply buying enough lottery tickets. The key that unlocks the door to opportunity is learning. **LEADERS ARE LEARNERS.** They learn from their failures as well as from their successes.

Here are some practical examples of challenging the process:

- A vice president of sales champions accessing a new market segment through a high-profile—and highly risky—executive conference.

- A new plant manager, who wants to communicate that "things are going to be different," has the floors cleaned, walls painted, and employee washrooms renovated so as to grab people's attention and make it clear that she's serious about getting started quickly.

- A marketing manager openly disagrees with her boss regarding plans for a new product launch.

- The leader of a team in a bank looking at how to enhance service sends team members to a department store known for its customer orientation so they can experience service quality there and bring back suggestions on how to apply those ideas at the bank.

Guidelines for Challenging the Process

Try these strategies to change, grow, innovate, and improve:

- Treat every job as an adventure.

- Send people shopping for ideas.

- Put "idea gathering" on your own agenda.

- Go out and find something that needs fixing.

- Take a class; learn a new skill.

- Experiment, experiment, experiment.

- Make it safe for *others* to experiment.

- Work with ideas that may sound strange initially.

- Debrief every failure as well as every success.

- Model risk taking.

S T O P   A N D   T H I N K

What "daring failure" have you experienced in your life? What did you learn? (Be specific.)

What is fun and rewarding about taking risks and trying new things?

What aspects of challenging the process may be difficult for you? Why?

STRETCHING THE LIMITS

When you described your personal best project in Worksheet One of the preceding chapter, you identified several aspects of the project that you expect to be frustrating or difficult. Such expectations reflect underlying assumptions that you or others might be making about various aspects of the project. These assumptions are likely to hold you back.

For example, suppose you wrote "tight time frame" as one aspect of the project that may be frustrating or difficult. Underlying, limiting assumptions could include:

Source of frustration	Limiting assumptions
Tight time frame	Inadequate staffing
	Inadequate budget for temps
	Other management priorities
	Too many other conflicting commitments

Review the potential sources of frustration you listed in Worksheet One. In the box below, write down any limiting assumptions you or others may hold about any aspects of this project.

Now fill out Worksheet Two, "Stretching the Limits."

STRETCHING THE LIMITS

In my personal best project:
How can I take the initiative to overcome obstacles?

How can I question the status quo?

Which we've-always-done-it-this-way processes could we reinvent to achieve the project goals?

How can I search outside the organization to discover unexpected ideas?

Examples: *Arrange a field trip that would stimulate our group's thinking.*

              Read magazines from fields I know nothing about.

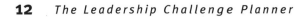

How can I experiment and foster risk taking? What daring experiments could our group undertake and learn from? How can I reward and encourage others to take risks on this project? How can I frame my project as an experiment, so that early efforts can clearly be seen as demonstrating lessons?

Behind every apparent limitation is an opportunity waiting to be discovered. Now we're going to ask you to think outside the box—literally! By doing so, you can transform how you approach any obstacle.

Look at this example of thinking (and writing) outside the box:

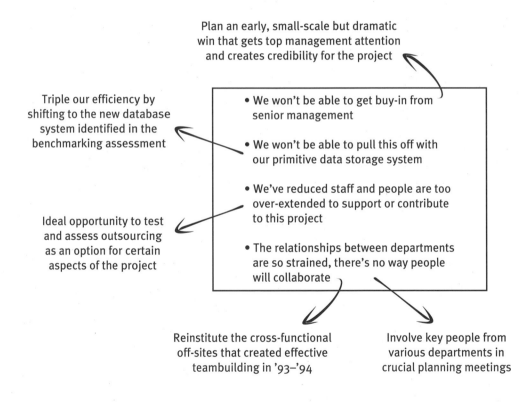

Plan an early, small-scale but dramatic win that gets top management attention and creates credibility for the project

Triple our efficiency by shifting to the new database system identified in the benchmarking assessment

Ideal opportunity to test and assess outsourcing as an option for certain aspects of the project

- We won't be able to get buy-in from senior management

- We won't be able to pull this off with our primitive data storage system

- We've reduced staff and people are too over-extended to support or contribute to this project

- The relationships between departments are so strained, there's no way people will collaborate

Reinstitute the cross-functional off-sites that created effective teambuilding in '93–'94

Involve key people from various departments in crucial planning meetings

Refer back to the list of limiting assumptions you wrote a moment ago in the empty box (p.10). To challenge the process, identify a way to turn each potential limitation into an opportunity to grow. Draw arrows from each limitation to a point outside the box as in the previous example, and write an opportunity for each limitation.

THE BOTTOM LINE

Drawing from the ideas kindled in this chapter, express your intention to commit yourself now to challenging the process in this project.

THE STATUS QUO I'll overturn:

EXPERIMENTS I'll try:

PLACES WHERE I'LL LOOK for new ideas:

WAYS IN WHICH I'LL REWARD failure:

IMMOVABLE OBSTACLES I'll demolish:

OTHER WAYS I'LL CHALLENGE the process:

4 Inspiring a Shared Vision

In describing to us their personal best leadership experiences, people told of times when they imagined an exciting, highly attractive future for their organization. They had visions and dreams of what *could* be. They had absolute and total personal belief in those dreams, and they were confident in their ability to make extraordinary things happen. Every organization, every social movement, begins with a dream. **THE DREAM OR VISION IS THE FORCE THAT INVENTS THE FUTURE.**

LEADERS INSPIRE A SHARED VISION. They gaze across the horizon of time, imagining the attractive opportunities that are in store once they and their constituents arrive at the final destination. Leaders have a desire to make something happen, to change how things are, to create something that no one else has ever created before.

In some ways, leaders live their lives backward. They see pictures in their mind's eye of what the results will look like even before they've started their project, much as an architect draws a blueprint or an engineer builds a model. Their clear image of the future pulls them forward. Yet a vision seen only by a leader is insufficient to create an organized movement or a significant change in a company. A person with no constituents is *not* a leader, and people do not follow until they accept a vision as their own. **LEADERS CANNOT COMMAND COMMITMENT; THEY CAN ONLY INSPIRE IT.**

To enlist people in a vision, you as a leader must know your constituents and speak their language. People must believe that the leader understands their needs and has their interests at heart. Only through an intimate knowledge of their dreams, hopes, aspirations, visions, and values are you able to enlist support. **LEADERSHIP IS A DIALOGUE**, not a monologue.

LEADERS BREATHE LIFE into the hopes and dreams of others and enable them to see the exciting possibilities that the future holds. Leaders forge unity of purpose by showing constituents how the dream is for the common good.

And as a leader, you don't ignite the flame of passion in others if you can't express enthusiasm for the compelling vision of the group. You must communicate your passion through vivid language and expressive style.

Without exception, the leaders in our study reported that they were incredibly enthusiastic about their personal best projects. Their own excitement was catching; it spread from leader to constituents. Their belief in and commitment to the vision were the sparks that ignited the flame of inspiration.

What is a vision?

We define vision as a unique and ideal image of the future for the common good.

As a practical example of an inspiring vision, here's a good one:

> *Over the next two years, we will work together to create fully integrated and interactive systems for financial tracking and reporting. From where we are today, that may seem like trying to build the Pyramids at Giza. It's a huge project, with a lot of pieces that have to come together smoothly, but it is possible.*
>
> *The basic policies and procedures we're putting in place today are the foundation stones. As we build each system, we'll be putting more stones in place. Then, merging and integrating the systems will be the "capstone" that completes this awe-inspiring accomplishment.*
>
> *Along the way, we may get discouraged—that there are too many stones, the stones are too heavy, there aren't enough of us. But I know that the organization is com-*

mitted to this project and will give us what we need to complete it. The final system will have all the elegance and durability of the pyramids. People will be able to access timely, relevant, reliable and secure information from their desktops. No more hounding for current numbers, and all the glitches that arise from systems that aren't integrated.

Picture their faces when . . .

The sales rep accesses current cost information from her laptop and beats the competitor's proposal by three days and 20 percent.

The service technician accesses accurate inventory data and can confidently promise delivery dates to a customer.

This is what we can—and will—create together. We will make it possible.

Guidelines for Inspiring a Shared Vision

Try these strategies to envision an uplifting future and enlist others in the vision:

- Determine what you want.
- Act on your intuition.
- Test your assumptions.
- Become a futurist.
- Develop your interpersonal competence.
- Breathe life into your vision.
- Speak positively.
- Speak from the heart.
- Make the intangible tangible.
- Listen, listen, listen.

What truly inspires you about your project?

Beyond its business or financial objectives, what higher meaning or purpose does (or could) this project serve?

What future trend(s)—demographics, technology, etc.—will affect the outcome of this project?

Envisioning the Future

Picture yourself, your team, and your organization at the end of this project. It has been successful beyond your wildest dreams. What do you see? Describe the details in Worksheet Three, "Envisioning the Future."

ENVISIONING THE *FUTURE*

What people are doing:

What people are saying:

What people are feeling:

What it smells like:

What colors I see:

Using Metaphor

The most powerful visions use metaphor or visual analogy to change abstract notions into tangible and memorable images. Here are possible metaphors for your project:

 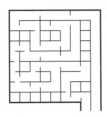

Take a few minutes to identify a concrete object or event that is analogous to your project, one that might be inspiring if your team and other stakeholders hold it in mind. Then make a few notes to help you really grasp and internalize just how this metaphor or visual analogy is similar to your project. To take one of the examples above:

Metaphor	**How it's like this project**
• Example: *Skyscraper*	*Ambitious, expensive*
	Reaching to the sky
	Requires a team and lots of coordination
	Requires different kinds of material to make it strong and beautiful
• Your metaphor:	•
	•
	•
	•
	•
	•

Enlisting Others

Now, take a few moments to think about the people whom you want your vision to inspire. Who are they? Be sure to include as many groups as you can identify: customers, shareholders, and vendors, as well as team members on your list. What motivates them? Write each audience and its key motivators in this figure:

Shareholders or owners
Profit
Future growth
Competitive advantage

Now review what you've written with one objective in mind: to identify what these audiences have in common. How can you appeal to their overlapping interests?

Vision Statement

As a culmination of all the thinking you've done in this section, you are now going to write a compelling vision statement for your project. Do you remember how we defined vision earlier in this chapter? If not, turn back to p. 18 to review it. Now use Worksheet Four, "Vision Statement," to make notes on the key components of your vision.

What *ideal* or passion inspires me and my constituents on this project?

What is *unique* about my dream for this project?

What *future* do I envision for my constituents and for
the greater organization or community?

How does this vision serve the *common good*: the good of all essential constituents?

What tangible *image(s)* can I provide that appeal to others?

Now pull all the pieces together and write your vision in a paragraph or two.

THE BOTTOM LINE

Which trusted friend or colleague can I approach to "test run" my vision? When specifically can I do it?

What are three public and private situations I can use to share all or part of my vision?

If people are already enlisted and committed, how will I know if they are genuinely inspired?

5 Enabling Others to Act

The individuals we studied for *The Leadership Challenge* recognized that a grand dream doesn't become significant reality through the actions of a single leader. **LEADERSHIP IS A TEAM EFFORT.** After reviewing twenty-five hundred personal best cases, we developed a simple (and highly informal) test to detect if someone is on the road to becoming a leader. The test: listen to the person and note how frequently he or she uses the word *we*.

Exemplary leaders enlist the support and assistance of all those who must make the project work. This sense of teamwork goes far beyond a few direct reports or close confidants. In today's "virtual" organization, cooperation can't be restricted to a small group of loyalists; it must include peers, managers, customers and clients, suppliers, citizens . . . in short, everyone who has a stake in the vision. **LEADERS INVOLVE,** in some way, all those who must live with the results, and they make it possible for others to do good work. *They enable others to act.* Leaders know that no one does his or her best when feeling weak, incompetent, or alienated; they know that those who are expected to produce the results must feel a sense of ownership.

LEADERS ENABLE OTHERS TO ACT not by hoarding the power they have but by giving it away. When people have discretion, authority, and information, they're likely to use these resources and their energies to produce extraordinary results.

In the cases we analyzed, leaders proudly discussed teamwork, trust, and empowerment as essential elements of their efforts. For constituents, too, a leader's ability to enable others to act is essential; in fact, from the constituents' vantage point, this is the most significant of the five practices. **LEADERSHIP IS A RELATIONSHIP,** founded on trust and confidence. Without trust and confidence, people don't take risks. Without risks, there's no change. Without change, organizations and movements die.

Here are practical examples of enabling others to act:

A vice president of property services is given the assignment to double available workstations at an already crowded facility—in nine months. In a series of meetings with his team, he asks them to evaluate alternatives and set a plan of action. Once the team does so, he entrusts them with implementing it. His role is to make sure people are organized, on schedule, and headed in the same direction. He also intervenes if teamwork breaks down or problems fall between the cracks. He provides lots of feedback throughout the process.

One manufacturing executive facing a possible plant closure trains all employees to read and interpret financial statements. The company's financial information is shared and discussed regularly—by machine workers and clerical staff as well as management. The company not only has avoided bankruptcy but has become consistently profitable by expecting everyone in the company to act as a business owner.

Guidelines for Enabling Others to Act

Try these strategies to build trust and strengthen others:

- Always say *we*.
- Increase interactions.
- Focus on gains, not losses.
- Form planning and problem-solving partnerships.
- Go first.
- Enlarge people's sphere of influence.
- Make sure delegated tasks are relevant.
- Make connections.
- Make heroes of other people.
- Educate, educate, educate.

Think of a time when you felt powerful as a result of something a manager said or did. Specifically, what did the manager do or say? How did you feel? Aside from empowered, how did you feel?

Think of a time when you felt powerless as a result of something a manager said or did. What specifically did he or she do? How did these actions make you feel?

Now, using the lessons you've learned from your own experiences, ask yourself: How can you enable others to feel powerful and avoid diminishing their personal efficacy?

Ask yourself: If I'm able to make others feel powerful, how can that accomplishment benefit this project?

Creating Power Profiles

Next we turn to a worksheet that we call the "power profile." Complete one profile for each person on your project team. Six forms are provided; if you need additional forms, feel free to make photocopies.

POWER PROFILE

Team member_____

Project role_____

What motivates this person?

What unique perspective does this person bring to our team?

Which of this person's strengths and skills can our team use?

What kind of training might help this person become a stronger team member?

What opportunities can I provide for this person to assume greater responsibility or achieve greater visibility?

What information does this person require to work productively?

What opportunities can I provide for this person to work collaboratively with other team members?

POWER *P R O F I L E*

Team member_____

Project role_____

What motivates this person?

What unique perspective does this person bring to our team?

Which of this person's strengths and skills can our team use?

What kind of training might help this person become a stronger team member?

What opportunities can I provide for this person to assume greater responsibility or achieve greater visibility?

What information does this person require to work productively?

What opportunities can I provide for this person to work collaboratively with other team members?

POWER *PROFILE*

Team member_____

Project role_____

What motivates this person?

What unique perspective does this person bring to our team?

Which of this person's strengths and skills can our team use?

What kind of training might help this person become a stronger team member?

What opportunities can I provide for this person to assume greater responsibility or achieve greater visibility?

What information does this person require to work productively?

What opportunities can I provide for this person to work collaboratively with other team members?

POWER *P R O F I L E*

Team member_____

Project role_____

What motivates this person?

What unique perspective does this person bring to our team?

Which of this person's strengths and skills can our team use?

What kind of training might help this person become a stronger team member?

What opportunities can I provide for this person to assume greater responsibility or achieve greater visibility?

What information does this person require to work productively?

What opportunities can I provide for this person to work collaboratively with other team members?

POWER PROFILE

Team member_____

Project role_____

What motivates this person?

What unique perspective does this person bring to our team?

Which of this person's strengths and skills can our team use?

What kind of training might help this person become a stronger team member?

What opportunities can I provide for this person to assume greater responsibility or achieve greater visibility?

What information does this person require to work productively?

What opportunities can I provide for this person to work collaboratively with other team members?

POWER PROFILE

Team member_____

Project role_____

What motivates this person?

What unique perspective does this person bring to our team?

Which of this person's strengths and skills can our team use?

What kind of training might help this person become a stronger team member?

What opportunities can I provide for this person to assume greater responsibility or achieve greater visibility?

What information does this person require to work productively?

What opportunities can I provide for this person to work collaboratively with other team members?

Review your team member power profiles. Identify at least one enabling action that you can take for the benefit of each person on the team. On the following page, indicate how you can help people connected to information.

Team member	**Enabling action(s)**
Example: *Bill*	*Put him in touch with Betty in Information Technology for systems assistance*

What systems can I establish to ensure that people have access to the information they need to succeed in this project?

6 Modeling the Way

Titles are granted and bestowed, but it's not your title that wins you respect. Your behavior does. You should never ask anyone to do anything that you're not willing to do first. **LEADERS GO FIRST.** They set an example and build commitment through simple, daily acts that create progress and momentum. **LEADERS MODEL THE WAY, THROUGH PERSONAL EXAMPLE AND DEDICATED EXECUTION.**

To model effectively as a leader, you must first **BE CLEAR ABOUT YOUR PRINCIPLES.** You are supposed to stand up for your beliefs, so you'd better have some beliefs to stand up for. Eloquent speeches about common values aren't nearly enough. Just as your behavior outweighs your title in constituents' eyes, so too your deeds are far more important than your words—and the actions must be consistent with the ideas.

The personal best projects we heard about in our research were all distinguished by relentless effort, steadfastness, competence, and attention to detail. **LEADERS NEED OPERATIONAL PLANS.** They must steer projects along a purposeful course, measure performance, give feedback, meet budgets and schedules, and take corrective action. Yet the personal best cases we examined included very little about grand strategic plans and massive organizational changes; actually, they sounded more like action adventure stories! They were tales about the power of little things, small advances, piling one on top of the other until they added up to something big. Concentrating on producing small wins, leaders build confidence that even the biggest challenges can be met. In so doing, they strengthen commitment to the long-term future.

Here are some practical examples of modeling the way:

> *The president of a chain of neighborhood convenience stores doesn't just talk about the importance of employee satisfaction and work-family balance. On*

important national holidays, he and other corporate office staff members work in the stores so that employees can spend time with their families.

The division manager of an electric and gas utility works diligently to demonstrate the importance of customers. She makes a point every day of bringing up customers in her daily interactions with other employees. The first agenda item in her staff meetings is always customer satisfaction.

A new superintendent is appointed for a school district in deep trouble: 50 percent of the schools are closed and 98 percent of the children are performing at the lowest percentile ranking by the state's education department. Her first step is to enlist community and business support to refurbish one particularly decrepit school. This initial success creates momentum for neighborhood pride and civic involvement that then proves unstoppable.

Guidelines for Modeling the Way

Try these strategies to set the example and achieve small wins:

- Open a dialogue about personal and shared values.
- Audit your actions.
- Be dramatic.
- Tell stories about teachable moments.
- Take personal interest in everything.
- Make a plan.
- Create a model.
- Break it up, and break it down.
- Ask for volunteers.
- Sell the benefits, benefits, benefits.

Imagine that it's one year after your project was successfully concluded. You overhear several people talking about the legacy you've left as a result of how the project was handled. What two or three things do you hope to hear them say?

What are you already doing to help create this legacy?

What do you need to start doing? What must you stop doing?

Values in Action

A value is defined as "something (as a principle or quality) intrinsically desirable."

Your values are the underlying priorities that guide your decisions. Because you hold many values, at times some of them are going to be in conflict with others. For example, let's say you identify a new technology that can increase your department's productivity, but it will probably result in some layoffs. In your decision process, you are likely to weigh such values as productivity and profitability against, say, loyalty, security, and respect for employees' family needs. For each individual, and in each situation, the equation is unique. Greater understanding of your values can lead to better and quicker decisions.

For this project, which values are most important to its successful completion? What themes or principles do you want everyone to understand and hold as priorities? Review the list we offer here of some commonly held business values, and select the five that you feel are most important in successfully completing your project. In the blank lines at the end of the list, add any values that you think are missing in your situation.

_____achievement   _____freedom   _____responsibility

_____caring   _____fun   _____risk

_____caution   _____growth   _____security

_____challenge   _____honesty and integrity

_____communication   _____human relationships _____speed

_____competition   _____individualism   _____task focus

_____cooperation   _____innovation   _____teamwork

_____creativity   _____involvement   _____uniqueness

_____curiosity   _____learning   _____winning

_____customer focus   _____organization

_____determination   _____productivity   _____ _____

_____diversity   _____profitability   _____ _____

_____fairness   _____quality   _____ _____

_____family time   _____quantity   _____ _____

_____flexibility   _____respect   _____ _____

For your key values to become meaningful guidelines for your team, you need to communicate them and model them to others. This process starts with clarifying for yourself what the words that you've chosen mean to you. In Worksheet Six, "Values in Action," take a few minutes to write a definition of each value you've chosen. Then describe what the value looks like in implementation, that is, in action. In other words, when people embrace this value, what do they do?

VALUES IN ACTION

Value	My definition	What it looks like in action
Example: *Customer focus*	• *Customers are our top priority; we must factor their needs in to every decision on this project*	• *Focus groups can be used at key milestones to guide our progress* • *Customer advisor on project team*
Value:	•	• • •
Value:	•	• • •

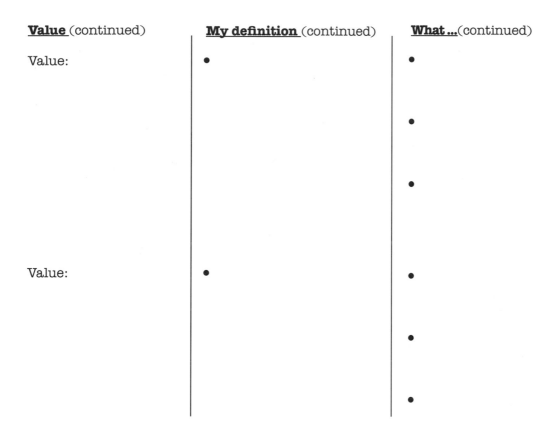

Value (continued)	**My definition** (continued)	**What ...**(continued)
Value:	●	●
		●
		●
Value:	●	●
		●
		●

As project leader, what can you do to demonstrate the importance of these values to the team, to colleagues, and to management? For each value, brainstorm two or three actions you can take to show your commitment to the value. Actions might include:

- How you spend your time
- How you deal with critical incidents
- Using metaphors to illustrate what the values mean
- Telling stories about exemplary actions by others
- Intentionally interacting and communicating with those who set an example
- Selecting symbols and following rituals
- What you reward people for
- Asking questions that probe key values

Think broadly and creatively here. You have a chance later to select actions you'll commit to taking.

Value	**Actions I'll take as leader**
Example: *Customer focus*	• *Include customer feedback at top of every project meeting agenda*
	• *Spend 25 percent of my time meeting with customers*
Value:	•
	•
	•
Value:	•
	•
	•
Value:	•
	•
	•

Achieve Small Wins

The second important aspect of modeling the way is achieving small wins that act as guide-posts along the way. By breaking your project down into manageable pieces, you provide focus to the team and a map of your progress. Review the sample map in the figure below.

	Milestone	Target Date
1	1st meeting: clarify roles	June 28
2	Create new marketing strategy	end July
3	Management approval	Aug 4–5 offsite
4	Educate sales force	Aug–Sept
5	Launch new campaign	Sept 15
6		
★	**Project Completion**	Celebrate! Sept. 18

Now chart your own map of project milestones on this page, showing small-win signposts and target dates or time frames. Include target date and key accomplishment(s) for each milestone.

Milestone   **Target Date**

1 _____   _____
  _____

2 _____   _____
  _____

3 _____   _____
  _____

4 _____   _____
  _____

5 _____   _____
  _____

6 _____   _____
  _____

Project Completion   _____

THE BOTTOM LINE

Review your values-in-action worksheet from this chapter (p. 44). For each of your top project values, select one action for you to take personally to demonstrate it. On the next page, plan a small win milestone.

Value   **Action I'll take personally**

Review your milestone map. What first step can you take right away to create a small win to move the project along?

7 Encouraging the Heart

The climb to the top is arduous and long. People become exhausted, frustrated, and disenchanted. They're often tempted to give up. **LEADERS ENCOURAGE THE HEART** so that their constituents carry on. If people observe a charlatan making noisy pretenses, they turn away. But seeing genuine acts of caring uplifts the spirit and draws people forward.

Encouragement can come from dramatic gestures or simple actions. It's part of the leader's job to **SHOW PEOPLE THAT THEY CAN WIN.** In the cases we collected, there were thousands of examples of individual recognition and group celebration: marching bands, bells, T-shirts, notecards, personal thank-yous, and a host of other awards to offer visible signs of encouragement to keep on winning. Recognition and celebration aren't just fun and games, however. **ENCOURAGEMENT IS A CURIOUSLY SERIOUS BUSINESS.** It's how leaders visibly and behaviorally link rewards with performance. As people strive to raise quality, recover from disaster, start up a new service, or make dramatic change of any kind, leaders make sure they benefit whenever behavior is aligned with cherished values.

In the cases we examined, we saw evidence not only of leaders encouraging others but also of leaders encouraging themselves. Love—of their products, their services, their constituents, their clients and customers, and their work—may be the best-kept leadership secret of all.

Here are two practical examples of encouraging the heart:

> *When his team reaches a key milestone, a project manager shakes the hand of each team member, takes several key team members to lunch, calls each*

team member to personally thank him or her for effort and contributions, and hosts a small cake-and-coffee celebration party.

A plant manager creates monthly "super person" award ceremonies in which she recognizes people who make special contributions to improving productivity or reducing costs. At each ceremony, she presents a creatively chosen, humorous gift that symbolizes what the person has done and tells the story of why that person is receiving the award.

Guidelines for Encouraging the Heart

Try these strategies to recognize individual contributions and celebrate team accomplishments:

- Seek out people who are doing things right.
- Personalize and publicize each recognition.
- Link the recognition to a clear set of standards.
- Celebrate individual recognition in a group.
- Be creative about rewards and recognition.
- Give recognition and rewards.
- Tell the story of someone who exemplifies the standards you set.
- Design the reward-and-recognition system participatively.
- Provide feedback en route.
- Schedule celebrations.
- Be a cheerleader, in your own preferred way.
- Stay in love with what you do.
- Have fun, laugh, enjoy.

Recall meaningful recognition that you've received. What elements made the fact of recognition (or the event, if such was the case) particularly meaningful?

How did you feel as a result of the experience?

Recognize Contributions

Recognizing an individual's job well done is your opportunity not only to encourage the heart of your team members but also to reinforce your project values. Refer back to Chapter Six, p. 44, where you described what each desired value looks like in terms of on-the-job behavior. The best way to generate more of the behavior you want is to watch for examples of people who are doing things right. Don't wait to say thank-you; recognize them as soon as possible.

As your project progresses, use Worksheet Seven, "Kudos for a Comrade," to think through how you can recognize any individual who makes a special contribution to the project by exemplifying one of the project values. Four copies are provided; copy more if necessary.

KUDOS FOR A COMRADE

Team member:_____

Value: _____

What has the team member done to exemplify the value?

How can I personalize the recognition? How can I customize and make the recognition special for this person?

Where and when will I recognize the person?

Who else should know about this? How can I publicize it to them?

KUDOS FOR A COMRADE

Team member:_____

Value: _____

What has the team member done to exemplify the value?

How can I personalize the recognition? How can I customize and make the recognition special for this person?

Where and when will I recognize the person?

Who else should know about this? How can I publicize it to them?

KUDOS FOR A COMRADE

Team member: _____

Value: _____

What has the team member done to exemplify the value?

How can I personalize the recognition? How can I customize and make the recognition special for this person?

Where and when will I recognize the person?

Who else should know about this? How can I publicize it to them?

KUDOS FOR A COMRADE

Team member: _____

Value: _____

What has the team member done to exemplify the value?

How can I personalize the recognition? How can I customize and make the recognition special for this person?

Where and when will I recognize the person?

Who else should know about this? How can I publicize it to them?

Celebrate Team Accomplishments

Every project milestone is an opportunity for the team members to celebrate what they've accomplished and then gather spirit and momentum to continue. For each of your project milestones (p. 48), brainstorm several fun and meaningful ways for people to celebrate as a team.

<u>**Project milestone**</u>	<u>**Team celebration**</u>
Example: *Create marketing strategy*	• *Stage a presentation of the strategy to rest of department; e.g., have team members "act out" the strategy in a skit*
	•
	•
	•

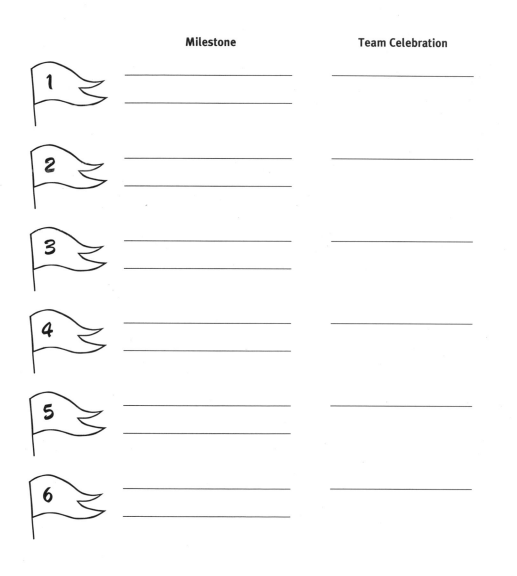

	Milestone	**Team Celebration**
1		
2		
3		
4		
5		
6		

THE BOTTOM LINE

Of all the leadership practices, encouraging the heart is the hardest to plan. Why? For one thing, you don't know in advance what people will do that merits recognition. For another, you want your recognition and celebrations to be spontaneous, genuine, and heartfelt. Too much planning can make recognition feel routine or forced.

Far from contrived or grin-and-bear-it acts of recognition, in this chapter you're laying the groundwork for creating a project that is filled with fun and meaningful celebration of "things gone right." You'll refer back to these pages often as you complete your weekly plans (Chapter Eight). As you practice encouraging the heart, frequent recognition and celebration become second nature.

To get started on encouraging the heart through effective recognition, here are two possible commitments for you to accept.

1. One person I'll recognize in the coming week:

   ■ Why:

   ■ How:

2. One celebration I'll hold within the next month:

   ■ Why:

   ■ How:

8 Designing Your Personal Best Project Plan

In the preceding pages, you've had the opportunity to delve deeply into the five practices of exemplary leadership and how they relate to your upcoming project. With some reflection, you've gained new insight and a broader perspective. These, in turn, have given rise to more focused intention on your part. By investing your time in this planner so far, you've demonstrated your commitment to transforming your project into a powerful leadership development experience (as well as an extraordinary success).

Now it's time to begin translating reflection and intention into *action*. This chapter helps you pull together your good ideas and considered intentions and set them into daily practice. This section of the *Planner* has two parts:

1. The grand plan. This integrating chart is your guide throughout the project. On it, you record your commitments to leadership action, organized by the project milestones you've already identified.

2. Weekly plans. As the project unfolds, you use these pages to create weekly leadership action commitments. Each weekly plan draws from the grand plan while incorporating what are certain to be new ideas, opportunities, and challenges that emerge along the way.

Instructions for the Grand Plan

Creating your grand plan is really simple—a three-step process.

First, transfer your project milestones and target dates (from your map in Chapter Six, p. 48) to the grand plan. Place them in order at the beginning of Worksheet Eight, "The Grand Plan," which appears later in this chapter.

Second, review the intentions you recorded for each leadership practice; they are on the closing pages, under the head "The Bottom Line," of Chapters Three through Seven (pp. 16, 26, 37, 49, and 60). Next, determine during which milestone you expect you will carry out each intention; transfer the intention to the grand plan worksheet in the appropriate milestone section.

Finally, review the other worksheet pages for any ideas you want to include in your grand plan (and, thereby, the weekly plans). We suggest that you examine in particular Worksheet One, My Personal Best Project, on p. 4; Five, Power Profile, on p. 31; and Seven, Kudos for a Comrade, on p. 54. Record these actions in Worksheet Eight in the same way.

Instructions for Weekly Plans

Each week, as your project progresses, prepare your weekly plan. It itemizes leadership actions you want to be sure to do in that week (see Worksheet Nine, "Weekly Plan"). As you transfer actions from the grand plan of Worksheet Eight, check them off to show they've been transferred. Then, as you complete each action on your weekly list, check it off as completed. Any action you are not able to complete should be transferred to the next week's plan, along with new ideas from the grand plan or ideas that evolve as you work with your team. (Make as many photocopies of Worksheets Eight and Nine as you need to cover the scope and duration of the project.)

Ideas for Energizing Commitment

With any project, unexpected factors may cause plans to change, team membership to shift, and deadlines to lengthen or shorten. We've kept the design of this planner as flexible and simple as possible to keep you from getting discouraged or losing focus. We also offer here some ideas for keeping alive your commitment to leadership development as time passes and pressures mount.

Set a Routine

Decide right now when you intend to prepare your plan for the upcoming week. Don't let a new week begin without having your plan ready.

Get a Buddy

Having a partner to compare notes with and confide in can be extremely helpful in keeping your focus and maintaining enthusiasm. Find a colleague who is willing to call or be called periodically to review leadership lessons and help think through any obstacles. Ideally, your partner is working on his or her own leadership development but is not involved in the same project with you.

Set Goals

Research indicates that people who set goals and get regular feedback perform better than those who do not. Your grand plan and weekly plans are a form of goal setting. In addition, set specific goals, such as:

I'll recognize someone publicly twice a week for the duration of the project.

I'll mention the project vision or some aspect of it at every project meeting.

Get Feedback

Actively seek input from colleagues, team members, and your manager regarding how you're doing. Welcome honest feedback, and keep your mind open to new perspectives. Being able to hear and respond constructively to feedback is an important part of becoming a leader.

Reassess

As you complete each milestone, reassess your grand plan and make necessary adjustments. What's working, and not working? What do you need to do more of, or less? What new people or challenges have arisen that require new action planning? What help do you need?

THE GRAND
P L A N

Milestone:_____ Target date:_____

 Challenging actions

 Inspiring actions

 Enabling actions

 Modeling actions

 Encouraging actions

THE GRAND P L A N

Milestone:_____Target date:_____

 Challenging actions

 Inspiring actions

 Enabling actions

 Modeling actions

 Encouraging actions

THE GRAND PLAN

Milestone:_____ Target date:_____

 Challenging actions

 Inspiring actions

 Enabling actions

 Modeling actions

 Encouraging actions

THE GRAND

P L A N

Milestone:_____Target date:_____

 Challenging actions

 Inspiring actions

 Enabling actions

 Modeling actions

 Encouraging actions

THE GRAND *P L A N*

Milestone:_____ Target date:_____

 Challenging actions

 Inspiring actions

 Enabling actions

 Modeling actions

 Encouraging actions

THE GRAND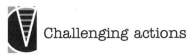

Milestone:_____Target date:_____

 Challenging actions

 Inspiring actions

 Enabling actions

 Modeling actions

Encouraging actions

WEEKLY P L A N

Milestone:_____Target date:_____

 Challenging actions

 Inspiring actions

 Enabling actions

 Modeling actions

 Encouraging actions

WEEKLY *PLAN*

Milestone:_____Target date:_____

 Challenging actions

 Inspiring actions

 Enabling actions

 Modeling actions

 Encouraging actions

WEEKLY P L A N

Milestone:_____ Target date:_____

 Challenging actions

 Inspiring actions

 Enabling actions

 Modeling actions

 Encouraging actions

WEEKLY *PLAN*

Milestone:_____Target date:_____

 Challenging actions

 Inspiring actions

 Enabling actions

 Modeling actions

 Encouraging actions

WEEKLY *P L A N*

Milestone:_____Target date:_____

 Challenging actions

 Inspiring actions

 Enabling actions

 Modeling actions

 Encouraging actions

WEEKLY

Milestone:_____Target date:_____

 Challenging actions

 Inspiring actions

 Enabling actions

Modeling actions

 Encouraging actions

WEEKLY P L A N

Milestone:_____Target date:_____

 Challenging actions

 Inspiring actions

 Enabling actions

 Modeling actions

 Encouraging actions

WEEKLY P L A N

Milestone:_____ Target date:_____

 Challenging actions

 Inspiring actions

 Enabling actions

 Modeling actions

 Encouraging actions

WEEKLY P L A N

Milestone:_____ Target date:_____

 Challenging actions

 Inspiring actions

 Enabling actions

 Modeling actions

 Encouraging actions

WEEKLY

Milestone:_____ Target date:_____

 Challenging actions

 Inspiring actions

 Enabling actions

 Modeling actions

Encouraging actions

WEEKLY P L A N

Milestone:_____ Target date:_____

 Challenging actions

 Inspiring actions

 Enabling actions

 Modeling actions

 Encouraging actions

WEEKLY *PLAN*

Milestone:_____Target date:_____

Challenging actions

Inspiring actions

Enabling actions

Modeling actions

Encouraging actions

WEEKLY PLAN

Milestone:_____Target date:_____

 Challenging actions

 Inspiring actions

 Enabling actions

 Modeling actions

 Encouraging actions

9 Reflecting on Your Personal Best Project

Throughout *The Leadership Challenge Planner*, you have been practicing reflection, intention, and action. Now that you've completed your personal best—or have achieved several significant milestones on the way to its completion—we encourage you to spend some time reflecting on your experience (that is, your intentions and actions). Remember, leaders are learners. To grow as a leader, you need to learn from your experiences so that you're ready to apply those lessons to your next project.

At the end of every project, many teams gather to debrief: to discuss what worked, what didn't, and what they learned. The questions in this final chapter take you through the debriefing process for your own project.

After answering each question, look closely. Ask yourself, *What does my answer reveal about my leadership style, about leading, and about how I can be more effective as a leader in the future?* Armed with the answers to these questions, you'll be ready to tackle your next personal best experience with better understanding and more thorough knowledge of your constituents and your strengths as a leader.

You may be finished with the execution of your landmark first personal best project, but the debriefing carries an even larger consequence: it's a critical step in the continuing process of your leadership development. Take the time to do it now, and reap the rewards for the rest of your leadership career.

My Personal Best Project

Review what you wrote in Worksheet One, "My Personal Best Project" (in Chapter Two), and answer these questions:

1. How well did you meet the project goals?

2. How well did your project meet your expected time frame? What about the budget?

3. How did you assess your progress? What criteria did you use?

4. Who else besides you evaluated your success? How did they measure it?

5. Which aspects of your project proved to be frustrating or difficult?

6. What surprised you along the way?

7. Think of several adjectives that describe how you feel about the project now (*proud, exhausted, fulfilled, excited . . .*).

8. How did the final outcome compare to your original assessment and feelings?

9. Overall, what have you learned about leadership that is new? What have you learned about yourself?

Challenging the Process

Review what you wrote in Worksheet Two, "Stretching the Limit," (in Chapter Three) and answer these questions:

1. What processes, systems, or structures did you change to achieve project goals?

2. What daring experiments did you try? How successful were they?

3. What have you learned about thinking outside the box?

4. What have you learned about challenging the status quo in your organization? Has the result been generally positive?

Inspiring a Shared Vision

Review what you wrote in Worksheets Three and Four, "Envisioning the Future" and "Vision Statement" (in Chapter Four), and answer these questions:

1. What higher purpose has this project served?

2. Review your vision statement; now that you've completed your project, how does the reality of what you've accomplished compare to what you envisioned? How does it differ? How do you account for the difference?

3. What metaphor would you use to describe this project now?

4. What did you learn about enlisting others in a shared vision? What have you learned about their hopes, dreams, and aspirations?

Enabling Others to Act

Review what you wrote in Worksheet Five, "Power Profile" (in Chapter Five), and answer these questions:

1. Which enabling actions have been the most successful?

2. Were the people on your team able to get the information they needed? What systems did you establish to ensure that this happened?

3. Write down some specific examples of when you gave power away. What effect did this have on your constituents? On you?

4. What did you do to make your constituents feel powerful? Was this task easier or more difficult than you expected? Why?

Modeling the Way

Review what you wrote in Worksheet Six, "Values in Action" (in Chapter Six), and answer these questions:

1. Did breaking down your project into small wins help you achieve your goals? Why or why not? How did doing so help, or hinder, progress?

2. How easy or difficult was it to forge consensus on values? Why do you think this was the case?

3. What values were the most important to you and your team in achieving your shared goals? How did *you* model these values?

4. What systems, structures, and processes needed to be changed so that you could create consistency between values and actions? What remains to be done?

Encouraging the Heart

Review what you wrote in Worksheet Seven, "Kudos for a Comrade" (in Chapter Seven), and answer these questions:

1. What form or forms of recognition have the most positive influence?

2. What was your most successful team celebration? Why was it effective?

3. What effect has recognition and celebration had on your team?

4. What creative means did you use to recognize individuals?

Tying It All Together

At last, it's time for some leisurely reflections on what you have learned overall in using *The Leadership Challenge Planner.*

1. What do you feel worked best with this project?

2. What surprised you?

3. What will you do differently next time?

4. What have you learned about yourself?

5. What have you learned about your constituents?

6. Which practice was the easiest to implement? The most difficult? Why?

7. (Very briefly, look ahead to the last three questions; then come back to this one.) What are your strengths as a leader? What weaknesses remain after the experience of this first personal-best leadership project?

8. Where do you need to improve your leadership skills?

9. What lessons have you learned about leadership from this experience?

10. How can you pass these leadership lessons on to others—especially to the next generation of leaders?

ALSO AVAILABLE FROM
JIM KOUZES AND BARRY POSNER

CREDIBILITY

Now available in paperback, *Credibility*—one of *Industry Week's* top ten management books of 1993—shows why leadership is above all a relationship, with credibility as the cornerstone. Best-selling authors Jim Kouzes and Barry Posner reveal six key disciplines and practices that work to strengthen a leader's capacity for development and sustaining credibility by relating rich examples and stories of real managers in action.

ISBN: 1–55542–550–X. *hardcover, 368 pages*

ENCOURAGING THE HEART

The best-selling authors of *The Leadership Challenge* team up again to reflect upon one of the most elusive aspects of leadership—caring—and offer readers a deeper understanding of how and why it works. More important, they extend a set of principles, practices, and examples that show how to energize people to excel and then reach for even greater heights.

ISBN: 0–7879–4184–0. *hardcover, 150 pages*

THE LEADERSHIP CHALLENGE

Second Edition

Completely revised and updated

With an expanded research base of 60,000 leaders, this second edition captures the continuing interest in leadership as a critical aspect of human organizations. It offers a broader scope of leaders in every industry and walk of life, including the education and nonprofit fields, and examines the era's hottest issues — the new cynicism, the electronic global village, evolving employee-employer relationships — in keeping pace with our ever-changing world.

ISBN: 0–7879–0110–5. *hardcover, 432 pages*
ISBN: 0–7879–0269–1. *paperback, 432 pages*

LEADERSHIP PRACTICES INVENTORY (2ND EDITION)

Second Edition

Leadership is learnable . . . and teachable!

Give your managers and supervisors the skills to master the Five Practices of Exemplary Leadership. Everything you need to obtain complete 360° feedback is included in this easy-to-use instrument.

LPI: Self ISBN: 0–7879–0970–X. *one 4–page instrument plus 96–page Participant's Workbook*
LPI: Observer ISBN: 0–7879–0972–6. *4 pages*
LPI Facilitator's Guide ISBN: 0–7879–0973–4. *includes a copy of LPI: Self, LPI: Observer, LPI Scoring Software*
LPI Deluxe Facilitator's Package ISBN: 0–7879–0988–2. *includes a copy of LPI Facilitator's Guide, Leadership Challenge (paperback)*

LEADERSHIP PRACTICES INVENTORY—INDIVIDUAL CONTRIBUTOR (LPI-IC)
Second Edition

Improve your leadership skills by using this powerful tool designed specially for nonmanagers—informal leaders and those involved in self-directed teams, project teams, task forces, and cross-functional teams.

LPI-IC: Self ISBN: 0–7879–0891–5. *one 4–page instrument plus 96–page Participant's Workbook*
LPI-IC: Observer ISBN: 0–7879–0982–3. *4 pages*
LPI-IC Facilitator's Guide ISBN: 0–7879–0983–1. *includes a copy of LPI-IC: Self, LPI-IC: Observer, LPI Scoring Software*

THE TEAM LPI
Create effective, high-performing work groups with *The Team LPI*!
Use this powerful instrument to help all your team members discover their leadership potential.

The Team LPI ISBN: 0–88390–313–X. *one 4–page instrument plus 24–page participant's manual*
The Team LPI Facilitator's Guide ISBN: 0–88390–541–8. *one Team LPI and Team LPI Facilitator's Guide (47 pages, paperback)*

THE STUDENT LEADERSHIP PRACTICES INVENTORY
This new version of Kouzes and Posner's tool for developing exceptional leadership is now tailored to the specific needs of students and young people! Appropriate for individual and group use, the assessment instruments can be used in any classroom, leadership development program, or with students and young adults in non-school settings.

Self-Instrument ISBN: 0–7879–4426–2. *NCR paper, 4 pages*
Observer Instrument ISBN: 0–7879–4427–0. *NCR paper, 4 pages*
Student Workbook ISBN: 0–7879–4425–4. *paperback, 24 pages*
Facilitator's Guide ISBN: 0–7879–4424–6. *paperback, 48 pages*
Facilitator's Package ISBN: 0–7879–4488–2. *includes Facilitator's Guide and one copy of each instrument*
Deluxe Facilitator's Package ISBN: 0–7879–4489–0. *includes Facilitator's Guide, one copy of each instrument, and one copy of* The Leadership Challenge *(paperback)*

WHAT FOLLOWERS EXPECT FROM LEADERS
How to Meet People's Expectations and Build Credibility
Leadership authors James Kouzes and Barry Posner provide concrete examples and specific guidance on how to become a more effective leader. Their unique format features stimulating interviews with corporate kingpins, a "drop–in" conversation with executives at a leadership seminar, and evocative questions directed at the reader.

ISBN: 1–55542–908–4. *two audiocassettes, two-hour running time*

LEADERSHIP CHALLENGE CARD
This handy, inexpensive pocket-sized card for desks, organizers, and wallets offers a quick reference to the Leadership Challenge model.

ISBN: 0–7879–4646–X. *pocket-sized card*

THE LEADERSHIP CHALLENGE PLANNER
An Action Guide to Achieving Your Personal Best
A practical implementation tool that takes users through the process of planning a major project using the Five Practices of Exemplary Leadership. This stand-alone, self-directed tool guides users through the planning and implementation of a personal best—that is, a leadership accomplishment with extraordinary results.

ISBN: 0–7879–4568–4. *paperback, 96 pages*

To order any of these Leadership Challenge resources, please contact your local bookstore, call Jossey-Bass/Pfeiffer at 1–800–956–7739, or visit our World Wide Web site at www.josseybass.com.